The Man
 Dinosaurs

by Katrina Van Horn

HOUGHTON MIFFLIN HARCOURT
School Publishers

ILLUSTRATION CREDIT: McEntee Art and Design

PHOTOGRAPHY CREDITS: Cover © Louie Psihoyos/CORBIS. 2 Siede Preis. 3 Associated Press. 4 Siede Preis. 5 © Richard T. Nowitz/CORBIS. 6 © Louie Psihoyos/CORBIS. 7 © 1997 PhotoDisc, Inc. 8 Laurie O'Keefe/Science Photo Library. (bkgd) © Getty Images. 9 Graham Rosewarne © Dorling Kindersley. (bkgd) © 1997 PhotoDisc, Inc. 10 © PhotoDisc, Inc. 11 Laurie O'Keefe/Science Photo Library. 12 Siede Preis. 13 Associated Press. 14 (bkgd) © PhotoDisc, Inc.

Printed in China

ISBN-13: 978-0-547-01734-1
ISBN-10: 0-547-01734-0

10 11 12 13 0940 18 17 16 15 14 13
4500443494

Jack Horner's Childhood

When he was a boy, Jack Horner wasn't good at math or reading. But he always loved science. He said his brain worked best when it could "hunt, poke, and dig around."

So when Jack Horner grew up, that's what he did. He became a paleontologist—a scientist who studies life from long ago. He spends his time digging around in the earth for clues about the past, especially clues about dinosaurs. He searches for dinosaur bones and other fossils—the remains of dinosaurs—to study and learn about these extinct beasts.

Horner grew up in Montana, a great location for fossil hunting. He and his father often searched for dinosaur bones buried in the hills near their home. Horner found his first dinosaur fossils when he was just eight years old!

Horner liked to look at every science book he could find. But he couldn't read any of them very well. In fact, he couldn't read *anything* very well. In high school he won every science fair with his projects, but he did poorly on science tests. He couldn't remember important facts. In college, he had the same kinds of problems. He learned a lot but still did badly on tests and couldn't read nearly as fast as the other students. So Horner did not graduate from college.

Jack Horner's Early Career

After he left school, Horner got a job in the Museum of Natural History at Princeton University. He worked on museum displays and did research. While he was at this job, he learned about a problem called dyslexia. People with dyslexia learn differently from other people. They have trouble reading and memorizing. Horner figured out that he had dyslexia. It was a big relief to understand why he had trouble in school, even though he was smart and tried hard.

During a summer vacation, Horner found the remains of dinosaur nests that contained the skeletons of baby dinosaurs. They were 75 million years old! No one had ever found anything like this before.

Soon after that, Horner began working at the
Museum of the Rockies back in Montana. He has now
been there for more than 25 years. The dinosaurs at
the museum include some that are 65 to 68 million
years old. They include famous dinosaurs such as
Triceratops (trie SER a tops), Tyrannosaurus rex
(ti RAN oh SAWR us REX), Ankylosaurus
(ANG ki lo SAWR us), and others.

Jack Horner holds the model of a baby Maiasaura as its model mother looks on.

Horner also began teaching at Montana State University. Because of his own learning problems, Horner said, "I never make my students memorize for tests. Instead, they have to explain what they know."

Horner has said that anyone interested in something should spend time doing it. "But do it your way. Don't worry about other people's expectations."

Jack Horner's Discoveries

One of Horner's most famous discoveries took place in 1978, when he unearthed a dinosaur no one had ever found before. Horner carefully studied the dinosaur's bones for clues about how the creature looked and lived. He figured out the dinosaur was a big, duck-billed plant-eater, or herbivore, that roamed around Montana about 77 million years ago.

Horner named the dinosaur Maiasaura (MAY ya SAWR a), which means "good mother lizard." He gave it that name because its bones were near nests containing remains of eggs and baby dinosaurs. Horner studied these nests and eggs carefully, too. He decided they were part of a colony where dinosaurs nested together year after year.

Horner knew that there were few plants to eat in the nest area. That information helped him figure out that the dinosaurs must have traveled to find food to bring back to their babies in the nest. Horner said this evidence helped prove that dinosaurs took good care of their babies—something scientists never understood before.

Maiasaura probably fed its babies in nests like birds do today.

In 1988, Horner discovered another dinosaur. He named this one Orodromeus (OR o DROHM ee us). After studying this dinosaur's bones, Horner concluded that it stood on two legs, grew quickly, and was able to search for its own food soon after it was born.

It was about eight feet long and probably stood no taller than a grown man. It likely spent its time running over mountainsides looking for plants to eat.

Then Horner made another huge discovery: the largest Tyrannosaurus rex, or T. rex, ever!

Horner found the fossil near five other T. rex fossils. He figured the dinosaurs may have been traveling in a pack when they died. That led him to wonder whether the T. rex was the fierce predator, or hunter, that it was long believed to be. Scavengers, or animals that eat the dead remains of other animals, are more likely to travel in packs. Predators often hunt alone.

Horner also thought that T. rex had poor vision and was a better walker than runner. He also thought its small arms would be pretty useless in a fight. This information seemed to fit in with his new hunch about T. rex.

Horner thinks that T. rex would have made an excellent scavenger, however. It had a great sense of smell, which would help it find dead animals. And its powerful teeth, while not very good at piercing meat, were perfect for crushing bones left behind by hunter dinosaurs.

Tyrannosaurus rex

Horner thinks that paleontologists have discovered less than one percent of the dinosaurs that once existed. But while other paleontologists focus on finding new species, Horner is much more interested in studying existing fossils.

Horner believes that learning what dinosaurs looked like is less important than gathering evidence about their behavior. For example, finding out about dinosaurs' family life, such as how they took care of their babies, can help scientists understand how other animals behave with their own mates and offspring.

Jack Horner's Awards

Horner's studies have helped give scientists a new way of looking at dinosaurs. Experts used to believe that dinosaurs were slow and not very smart. But now they know that many dinosaurs were fast, intelligent creatures that were much better at adapting to their environment than anyone had imagined. They did manage to survive for more than 140 million years, after all!

Horner received a MacArthur Foundation Award, which is also called the "Genius Award." The award is given to people who do important work in their field, or area of expertise. He also got an honorary degree from the University of Montana in 1986.

Horner has had another very special honor.
Two dinosaur species have been named after him:
Achelousaurus horneri (ak eh LOH uh SAWR us
HORN er ee) and Anasazisaurus horneri (ahn ah SAH
zee SAWR us HORN er ee). Not too many people can
hope for that in their lifetime!

Horner was also the real-life model for the lead
character, Dr. Alan Grant, in the movie *Jurassic Park*.
Horner helped the movie's director, Steven Spielberg,
make the dinosaurs in the movie look lifelike. If
you've seen *Jurassic Park*, you know he succeeded.
Those dinos are mighty fierce creatures!

These days, when he isn't studying fossils, Horner helps kids learn to love science. He tells children who visit the Museum of the Rockies that it's okay to argue with him about his ideas, and he tells them to gather evidence to back up their arguments. He has said, "The most important thing you can do is to teach children that it's just as okay to be wrong as it is to be right, because you never know if you're right."

Horner has two favorite kinds of dinosaurs. One is Maiasaura and other duck-billed dinosaurs. And the other? Well, one look at the license plate on his pickup truck will give you a clue.

Responding

Conclusions What text clues helped you draw conclusions, or make smart guesses, about Jack Horner? Copy the chart below. Write two more clues and the conclusion you can make from the clues.

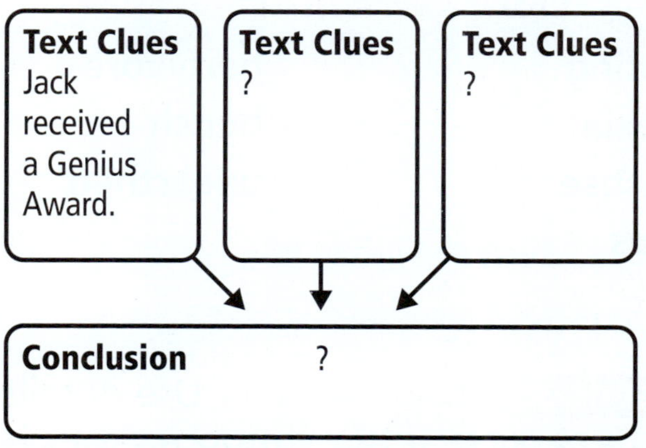

Write About It

Text to Self Write a paragraph that gives your opinion about whether looking for fossils is important work. Support your opinion with reasons and facts.

buried
clues
evidence
fierce
fossils

location
prove
remains
skeletons
uncovering

adapting
dyslexia
expertise
genius

herbivore
hunch
unearthed

TARGET SKILL **Conclusions** Use details to figure out ideas that the author doesn't state.

TARGET STRATEGY **Visualize** As you read, use selection details to picture what is happening.

GENRE **Informational text** gives factual information about a topic.